THE
MANAGING CHANGE
POCKETBOOK

3rd Edition

By Neil Russell-Jones

Drawings by Phil Hailstone

"Thought-provoking, balanced and practical guide for anyone involved in change - a 'must' for today's organisational life"
Cathryn Riley, Operations Director, General Insurance, Norwich Union

Published by:

Management Pocketbooks Ltd
Laurel House, Station Approach, Alresford, Hants SO24 9JH, U.K.
Tel: +44 (0)1962 735573   Fax: +44 (0)1962 733637
E-mail: sales@pocketbook.co.uk
Website: www.pocketbook.co.uk

First published 1995. Second edition 2003 ISBN: 978 1 903776 11 7.
This revised edition 2011 ISBN: 978 1 906610 39 5

E-book ISBN: 978 1 908284 19 8

British Library Cataloguing-in-Publication Data – A catalogue record for this book is available from the British Library.

Design, typesetting and graphics by **efex ltd**.   Printed in U.K.

ORDER FORM

Your details

Name _____

Position _____

Company _____

Address _____

_____

_____

Telephone _____

Fax _____

E-mail _____

VAT No. (EC companies) _____

Your Order Ref _____

Please send me:

	No. copies
The <u>Managing Change</u> Pocketbook	
The _____ Pocketbook	
The _____ Pocketbook	
The _____ Pocketbook	

Order by Post
MANAGEMENT POCKETBOOKS LTD
LAUREL HOUSE, STATION APPROACH,
ALRESFORD, HAMPSHIRE SO24 9JH UK

Order by Phone, Fax or Internet
Telephone: +44 (0)1962 735573
Facsimile: +44 (0)1962 733637
Email: sales@pocketbook.co.uk
Web: www.pocketbook.co.uk

Customers in USA should contact:
Management Pocketbooks
2427 Bond Street, University Park, IL 60466
Telephone: 866 620 6944 Facsimile: 708 534 7803
Email: mp.orders@ware-pak.com
Web: www.managementpocketbooks.com

MANAGEMENT POCKETBOOKS

About the Author

Neil Russell-Jones BSc (Hons), MBA, ACIB is an author and a management consultant and is a member of the Strategic Planning Society.

He works globally with many organisations in many countries assisting executives in developing or testing strategy, in improving their performance, change/programme management and in market analysis/research.

He has written many books and papers on business topics. His other titles include for Management Pocketbooks: *Business Planning, Decision-making, Strategy,* and *Marketing*; and for the Institute of Financial Services: *Customer Relationship Management, Risk Evaluation, Customers and Their Needs* and *Marketing, Sales and Customer Service*.

He has been a lecturer on the CASS EMBA course, and a special advisor for the Prince's Youth Business Trust (patron HRH the Prince of Wales) in the areas of strategy and marketing. Neil is a regular speaker in many countries and has often appeared on radio and TV.

You can contact him at neil.jones@eponaconsulting.com.

INTRODUCTION

DON'T BE A DINOSAUR

There are two ways of dealing with change:

- **Reactively** by responding only when you have to – often too late
- **Proactively** by anticipating it and planning to keep, if not one step ahead, then at least in the vanguard of change, and therefore able to minimise the downsides, or even to take advantage of it

Of course there is another option – ignore the change and hope it will go away. This was the course followed by the dinosaurs, dodos and many companies that couldn't read the writing on the wall (eg the British motorbike industry, devoured by the onslaught of Japanese companies). In similar vein, many companies globally are suffering from competition from Chinese exporters, as that economy leaps forward.

Any change, of course, must be managed properly or you can destroy what you have. For example, GEC decided to change from being basically a manufacturer into a telecoms company via a risky acquisition, and for good measure changed its name to Marconi to reflect this; just as the telecoms market collapsed: thus ruining a perfectly good company.

WHY READ THIS BOOK?

Just about everyone has been involved in change – either as a participant in a change programme, as a person directly affected or as someone indirectly touched by change.

For most of us, therefore, *change is now business as usual*. Change programmes are, however, by their nature difficult and complex. The change itself, and sometimes the reasons behind it, can be difficult to understand.

The objective of this book is to give you an understanding of the key elements in any change process, the issues, the pitfalls and then how to manage or avoid them.

You may be deeply involved in change, affected by it, or on the periphery; or you may just wish to understand the process a little more. This book will not make you into a change expert but will give you the basics and serve as an introduction into the process. The more you understand change, the better able you will be to cope with or manage it.

Dinosaurs died out!
Mammals did not!
Instead they embraced
change and survived.

CONTENTS

WHAT IS CHANGE?

WHAT IS CHANGE?

DEFINITIONS

Noun - Making or becoming different
- Difference from previous state
- Substitution of one for another
- Variation

Verb - To undergo, show or subject to change
- To make or become different

The emphasis is on making something different. This could be a major change or merely incremental.

SNOW WATER ICE STEAM

ANNUAL CHANGE CYCLE

There is major change all around you.

Each year the earth's rotation around the sun causes enormous change (more perceptible the further you are from the equator) known to us as 'seasons'. This change forces staggering responses; some trees (deciduous) drop their leaves and in effect close down for winter to bloom again in spring; some animals change their coats from summer to winter – eg mink/ermine – others, eg bears, hibernate for months.

Humans too have had to respond to climate changes and still do – by varying our clothing in season, or by using central heating or air conditioning. Our survival as a species has depended on our ability to adapt to major change, for example by using animal skins; our mastery of fire; or our use of collective irrigation to manage floods and droughts.

SPRING SUMMER FALL/AUTUMN WINTER

INCREMENTAL CHANGE

Sometimes, though, change creeps up in small stages – eg the change from the initial method of information storage, writing, to modern PCs with advanced capability and functionality, has been enormous; but took place over many, many years.

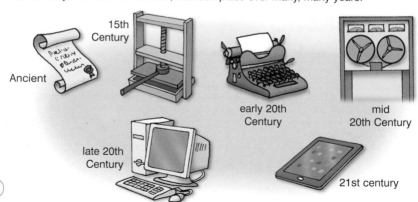

Ancient

15th Century

early 20th Century

mid 20th Century

late 20th Century

21st century

INCREMENTAL CHANGE

Each change built on the previous one; requiring new skills, training and capital outlay as well as new ways of working. More recently the pace and scale of change, in this area in particular, has increased exponentially; along with the implications, that are far-reaching and global. For example, it is now easy to work remotely from virtually anywhere in the world – a concept that was almost unimaginable, or at least not feasible, just a few years ago.

You can now download papers and books onto iPads, Kindles and other such devices instantly and carry hundreds of books; or thousands of songs in tiny machines, that will fit in the palm of your hand.

METAMORPHOSIS

Change can be of an even greater nature.
Consider metamorphosis, for example,
which requires a complete change of
state and represents a severe shock
to the status quo (in this case
requiring a sleeping phase to
cope with the change).

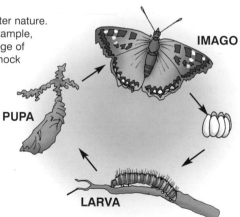

IMAGO

EGGS

LARVA

PUPA

WHAT IS CHANGE?

ORGANISATIONAL

- Almost every organisation has undergone change in the last 20 years – whether it was incremental or deep; desired or imposed

- The response to it and how change is managed should be in proportion to the depth of the change (see Depth of Change table following)

  ► For *slight change* a small (but still considered) response and effort is correct

  ► With *medium change* the change programme will be greater, involving more staff and resources and touching a great many

  ► For the *greatest change* then the programme may well be huge, absorb many other projects and also be the focus of the senior management for some time

- In all cases change must be analysed and understood and then a measured, planned and proportionate programme introduced to manage it

DEPTH OF CHANGE*

One way to understand change is to look at how it affects the organisation.

Graze	Fine-tuning - focus on efficiency
Surface	Restructure, reallocate resources
Shallow	Improve/change planning, slight change in thinking
Shift	Change CEO/MD, CEO/MD style, strategy
Penetrating	Change the organisation's definition of success, targets, goals
Deep	Change the vision, philosophy and mission
Deepest	Paradigm shift - change how you think, how problems are solved, how we do business

* After Huczynski & Buchanan

WHAT IS CHANGE?

MOVING FROM NOW TO THE FUTURE

Change management is the process of moving an organisation from where it is now to where it needs to be. This requires a transition that typically involves pain for some or, more commonly, many.

| CURRENT | TRANSITION | VISION |

Known Steady State **Pain/Change** **Unknown (unwanted by some)**

CHANGE IN BUSINESS

Not only must you have a good understanding of the change – it is absolutely necessary to answer the following questions:

Where are we going?	Clear, unambiguous vision
What will we look like when we get there?	How do we know that we have achieved the change?
What must be true to ensure we reach our goal?	What must we do, and what steps, implications, actions, resources and outputs are involved in order that we arrive at our destination?

WHAT DRIVES CHANGE?

There are many drivers, both internal and external, that drive change.

WHAT IS CHANGE?

WHAT DRIVES CHANGE?

What doesn't drive change is the attitude that, *'if it ain't broke don't fix it!'*

Yes – it may be working now – but will it work sufficiently
well in the future, given the scale and pace
of change that we experience daily?

*Adapt or die.
Copy, match or
innovate*

CHANGE DRIVERS

Factors driving change include:

- The appointment of new management: the 'new broom sweeps clean'
- Competition may force it, eg: home delivery of fast food (pizza), direct insurance sales or banking
- Loss of business confidence. For example, the collapse of Enron and Worldcom had unimagined implications. In particular, it destroyed Arthur Andersen & Co., one of the largest accounting firms in the world which had audited both companies. Its destruction occurred *virtually overnight*, as its reputation and brand were so damaged clients refused to deal with the firm. Staff lost their jobs or moved to other firms en masse
- The internet has had, and will continue to have, profound implications for all industries and has turned many upside down. In some cases the entire infrastructure has been radically altered (online financial services and shopping) and it has greatly facilitated home working, causing huge changes to work practices, travel and fixed asset needs. The results are all too apparent in the UK high streets with many well-known retail chains forced into administration, increasing numbers of 'to let' boarded up sites, and a proliferation of charity shops

BURNING PLATFORM

Typically there must be a 'burning platform' to cause the change to accepted practices.

This phrase comes from the Piper Alpha disaster in the North Sea where the only survivors were those who leapt off the rig **in defiance of instructions** and into the sea which was freezing cold and alight with oil. The burning platform forced a reappraisal of existing rules and the status quo.

For a company the burning platform is often a combination of things or one overriding concern – ie rising costs/falling revenue; liberalisation of rules thereby increasing competition or eroding margin; nationalisation – eg in the UK RBS and Lloyds/HBOS; or impending privatisation. For the newsprint industry there is a major issue with the low costs of electronic news versus the high expense of physical newspapers. One UK paper, the Guardian, has announced that it will be ceasing to produce its print edition at some future time. Others are expected to follow suit.

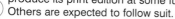

WHAT IS CHANGE?

SELF HELP

- For your organisation, list all the reasons **WHY** it might need to change
  Then rank them in order of priority/magnitude
- Now re-visit the list and ask **HOW** it would have to change to meet the **WHY**

WHY
we must change

Understanding

HOW
we must change

WHAT IS CHANGE?

WHY CHANGE?

EXAMPLES

Life company

- **Why**

  ▶ Increasing competition from banks and direct sales operations
  ▶ Losses pressurising capital reserves/profits
  ▶ Changing life expectancy and demographics as more people live longer

- **How**

  ▶ Reappraise distribution channels
  ▶ Reduce expenses as percentage of costs
  ▶ Offer new/ change existing products

WHAT IS CHANGE?

WHY CHANGE?

EXAMPLES

Manufacturer

- **Why**
  - ► Cheaper overseas producers
  - ► Technological developments render products obsolete (eg, CD:LPs, DVD:videos, iPod: walkman, iPads:Laptops)
  - ► New environmental rules

- **How**
  - ► Review overheads, invest in better assets/outsource production
  - ► Develop new products/ joint ventures
  - ► Review and change existing products

WHAT IS CHANGE?

WHY CHANGE?

EXAMPLES

Retailers

- **Why**

  ▶ Climate changes – eg less demand for fur, coal, coats – more summer wear, increased demand for BBQs, patio furniture
  ▶ Out-of-town/discount outlets taking trade from high streets
  ▶ Internet competition

- **How**

  ▶ Bring out new products, promote counter-cyclical products as 'fashion'
  ▶ Loyalty cards, form/join town loyalty schemes – take space at outlet sites
  ▶ Develop internet presence – use outlet chains for convenient collections rather than delivery; develop new logistics, distribution and delivery channels

PREPARING FOR CHANGE

PREPARING FOR CHANGE

MAKING IT HAPPEN

Making change happen involves:

- Moving an organisation's
  - ▶ people, and
  - ▶ culture

- In line with an organisation's
  - ▶ structure   ▶ strategy
  - ▶ processes   ▶ systems

Such that change is successful and delivers long-lasting benefit to the organisation!

This is not easy and, therefore, requires a process to assist in the management.
This is what **Change Management** is all about.

SUCCESSFUL CHANGE MANAGEMENT
COMMITMENT

Successful change management is about **taking the people with you**.

DOCK

HMS ORGANISATION

VISION /
OPPORTUNITY

Unless the people in an organisation – at all levels, from senior management to
employees – are committed to the change, **then it will fail**. This is not an option and
without this commitment any project is doomed.

SUCCESSFUL CHANGE MANAGEMENT

POSITIONING

It is important that a project is positioned correctly with respect to the organisation's culture and to people's beliefs and attitudes.

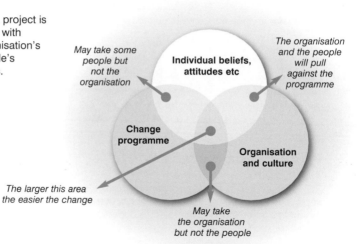

May take some people but not the organisation

Individual beliefs, attitudes etc

The organisation and the people will pull against the programme

Change programme

Organisation and culture

The larger this area the easier the change

May take the organisation but not the people

SUCCESSFUL CHANGE MANAGEMENT

EXPERT VIEWS

Much research has already been carried out into change.

Several management gurus are recognised; many have distilled their findings down to a number of key points.

Their findings, outlined on the following pages, are not cast in tablets of stone but do serve as useful reminders.

CONDITIONS FOR SUCCESS

EXPERT VIEWS

Rosabeth Moss Kanter was a professor at Harvard when she carried out research into change.

These are her 10 Commandments:

1. Analyse the organisation and its need for change
2. Create a shared vision and common direction
3. Separate from the past
4. Create a sense of urgency
5. Support a strong leadership role
6. Line up political sponsorship
7. Craft an implementation plan
8. Develop enabling structures
9. Communicate and involve people
10. Reinforce and institutionalise change

What she is saying is:

- ▶ Look at what you have got
- ▶ Obtain buy-in at all levels
- ▶ Plan the change, and
- ▶ Put in place a structure for implementing it
- ▶ Finally, make people live and breathe change

CONDITIONS FOR SUCCESS

EXPERT VIEWS

Conner Partners®, an American company established by Daryl Conner and specialising in change management, has built up an extensive database on change. Its four determinants are:

1 Sponsor commitment

2 Agent skills

3 Target resistance

4 Cultural alignment

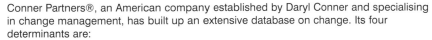

Main factors:

▶ Ensure that there is someone championing change who is empowered to make it happen

▶ Put people in place to make it happen

▶ Concentrate on those who resist most (the other side of the change bell curve – see diagram on page 92)

▶ Try to make the changes in accordance with usual practice, to make people feel as comfortable as possible

31

CONDITIONS FOR SUCCESS

EXPERT VIEWS

Beckhard, erstwhile professor at M.I.T. (USA), notes seven conditions for success:

1. Organisational vision and direction towards the vision
2. A clear sense of the organisation's identity
3. Understanding of the organisation's external relationships
4. Clear and reachable scenarios
5. Flexible structures
6. Effective use of technology
7. Rewards that harmonise people with the organisation's objectives

The key points here are:

▶ Understand your organisation and its relationships

▶ Be flexible

▶ Have a vision, and

▶ A map to get there

CONDITIONS FOR SUCCESS
SUMMARY OF EXPERT VIEWS

Each of the gurus has examined change and broadly come to the same conclusions:

- It is very difficult
- The further you go the harder it becomes
- The less that the change has in common with the organisation's culture, the less likely success is (or the harder you will have to work to get there)
- It needs a strong, important, organisationally powerful sponsor
- A body of people dedicated to making it happen is essential
- Communication is the key

CONDITIONS FOR SUCCESS
AIDE MEMOIRE

Make sure that your programme is a **SUCCESS** by following these key principles:

 S hared vision

U nderstand the organisation

C ultural alignment

C ommunication

E xperienced help where necessary

S trong leadership

S takeholder buy-in

CONDITIONS FOR SUCCESS

THE 'SUCCESS' PRINCIPLE

Shared vision

Ensure that there is a clear statement as to where the change is taking you and that this is understood by all stakeholders and makes sense

CONDITIONS FOR SUCCESS

THE 'SUCCESS' PRINCIPLE

Understand the organisation

Analyse the organisation to determine its key characteristics and those that need special attention

CONDITIONS FOR SUCCESS
THE 'SUCCESS' PRINCIPLE

Cultural alignment

Ensure that change is made in ways that are as close as possible to the *'way that things are normally done around here'*, unless this is not in the interests of the changes you wish to make

CONDITIONS FOR SUCCESS
THE 'SUCCESS' PRINCIPLE

Communication

Communicate as soon as there is something to say – to the right stakeholders in the right way (see Communication chapter)

CONDITIONS FOR SUCCESS
THE 'SUCCESS' PRINCIPLE

Experienced help where necessary

Use appropriate methodologies that
have been tried and tested to ensure
that your programme will deliver what you want;
if this means using external help then do so

CONDITIONS FOR SUCCESS

THE 'SUCCESS' PRINCIPLE

Strong leadership

A strong individual at the highest level appropriate must sponsor the change and be seen so to do. This individual must be seen to be dedicated to one goal: success of the programme and should have both organisational credibility and power to 'make it so'

CONDITIONS FOR SUCCESS
THE 'SUCCESS' PRINCIPLE

Stakeholder buy-in

Ensure buy-in from anyone with a stake in the success of the programme.

These may include:
employees, management, government, suppliers, lenders, owners

BARRIERS

A change programme will affect the way an organisation works. Two factors must be considered **before** implementation:

- **Culture – how an organisation operates**
  The change programme will almost certainly be counter cultural in some way

- **People – their reactions**
  How people will receive the change and the actions they might take to resist it

The two are inextricably linked.

Where barriers exist, they must be negated, avoided or climbed over. This means understanding the culture, readiness to change and the people.

PREPARING FOR CHANGE

BARRIERS

A survey conducted by William Schiemann and Associates Inc. in the USA found that the biggest obstacles to change were, in descending order of priority:

- Employee resistance
- Inappropriate culture
- Poor communication/plan
- Incomplete follow-up
- Lack of management agreement on strategy
- Insufficient skills

Another survey (Buchanan, Claydon, Doyle) found that where change initiatives had been instigated people agreed that:

- 63% felt 'initiative fatigue'
- 67% felt that there had been so much change, with few benefits, that most people were cynical about benefits
- 72% were suffering from information overload
- 78% felt that fear of the unknown was a major cause of resistance to change

PREPARING FOR CHANGE

WHAT IS CULTURE?

Culture is:
- The way that things are done in an organisation (or nation)
- What is acceptable and what is not
- Overt and covert rules/mores/norms that guide behaviour

Compare:
- ▶ savings bank
- ▶ investment bank

- ▶ civil service
- ▶ retail organisation

- ▶ nationalised company
- ▶ privatised company (in same sectors)

- ▶ Anglo-Saxon
- ▶ Continental

- ▶ Japanese
- ▶ Islamic

PREPARING FOR CHANGE

WHY LOOK AT CULTURE?

It is important to understand the culture of an organisation in order to understand how best to implement change.

These are some key indicators:

Modes of dress	(informal, dark suits in the City, less formal suits elsewhere, company uniform)
Attitudes	(helpful, couldn't care less, aggressive)
Styles of office/layout	(marble banking halls, pristine clear desks, piles of paper, open plan)
Types of buildings	(modern, old fashioned, expensive, poorly maintained)
Types of employees	(graduates, manual workers, creative, scientists)
Style of working	(clocking on, long hours, extensive travel, etc)

KEY ELEMENTS OF CULTURE

The key elements that influence culture include:

History	(long-established, new, product of mergers and acquisitions)
Ownership	(entrepreneurial, partnership, institution, State, many small shareholders, family, co-operative)
Operating environment	(global, national, regional, local)
Mission	(profit, charity, growth, value/price, quality, mutuality)
People	(graduates, manual workers, multi-national, accountants, actuaries, salesmen)
Management style	(paternal, hire and fire, benevolent, despotic, sharing, controlling)
IT	(how relevant is Information Technology to the industry - farming versus telecoms?)

CULTURAL AWARENESS

- It is the blend of these key elements, which differ for all entities, that make up the culture of an organisation; and in return may also reflect and reinforce that culture

- The programme must therefore analyse and understand these components to ensure that the correct elements are targeted to support success

We don't do things like that around here!

Failure to take culture into account will result in just that - failure - no matter how well planned and executed the change programme may be.

TYPES OF CULTURE

Charles Handy in his book `Understanding Organizations' identifies four main types of organisational culture:

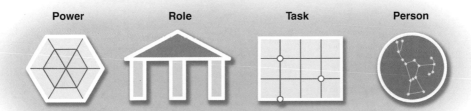

Power   Role   Task   Person

TYPES OF CULTURE

Power

This is symbolised by a web, as power flows along the lines to the centre, rather like the vibrations in a spider's web.

Power is wielded by individuals at the centre (eg: well-established entrepreneurial companies or a political party); decisions are easy but may not be right.

Key levers

To change the organisation, you must get the support of the central authority.

PREPARING FOR CHANGE

TYPES OF CULTURE

Role

This is symbolised by a Greek temple, because it is based on functional silos and is a very common type where communication flows up (in varying degrees) but never or seldom across (bureaucracy).

Stability is key, but it is vertical not horizontal. If this is lost eg through a poorly managed change programme – then the whole edifice can come tumbling down, rather like old Greek temples in an earthquake.

Key levers

To change this organisation you need to work up each 'leg' of the temple, following structure and protocol. This is time consuming, and is easier if you have a management structure looking across and down the whole organisation.

TYPES OF CULTURE

Task

This is symbolised by a net, as power flows up, across and down in a matrix structure.

Jobs are project or task oriented and very flexible with no structure.

Consultancies and some innovative companies are like this; a key feature is customer focused objectives.

Key levers

To change this organisation, you must take the key decision makers with you and gain buy-in from most members. This style of culture is more likely to respond to well-thought-out change.

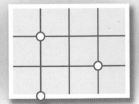

TYPES OF CULTURE

Person

This is symbolised by a cluster or constellation, as individuals are important. Such an organisation is rare and difficult to manage. Some partnerships are like this and professors within academia also fit this profile, getting on with their own interests, taking time out to meet organisational needs.

Key levers

To change this organisation, you must effectively take everyone with you.

PREPARING FOR CHANGE

CULTURE: ORGANISATIONAL ANALYSIS

Describe below the main symbols that reflect the culture of your organisation in terms of:

Modes of dress

Attitudes

Style of office

Buildings

Employees

Style of working

CULTURE: ORGANISATIONAL ANALYSIS

Then analyse your organisation and decide which one of the four cultural examples best fits:

		✔
Power	⬡	☐
Role	🏛	☐
Task	▦	☐
Person	◔	☐

This will enable you to understand the **key levers** that will need to be moved if undertaking change.

NB: This is a simple illustrative exercise, and more detailed analysis is necessary in a full change programme.

PEOPLE

HOW THEY REACT

- People react differently to change depending on their own personal circumstances and their understanding of the process
- Those opposed to change obviously need attention, but...
- Even those in favour of change will be affected and need to be managed properly

Understand the 'audience'

PREPARING FOR CHANGE

PEOPLE

NEGATIVE RESPONSE

Why do people have a negative response to change?

- They cannot see the point of the change (eg: the old guard who have been there for a long time and think everthing is OK)
- They are too busy (shooting the alligators to help in draining the swamp)
- They are threatened by the change (directly/indirectly)
- They **perceive** that they are threatened by the change (communication)
- Their politics make them natural enemies of the change
- There are cultural problems

Part of change management is identifying these problems and planning to negate them or obviate them.

PEOPLE

NEGATIVE RESPONSE

A negative response to change is to be expected. Change is different and many people will be against it on principle, whatever it actually means for them.

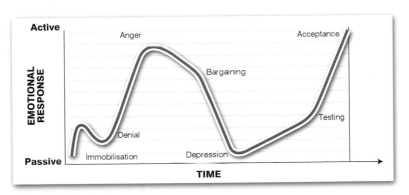

PEOPLE

NEGATIVE RESPONSE

A negative response to change is, in many respects, similar to grieving for the loss of a loved one. The difference may be in the timing and the difficulty of accepting the change; but the emotional responses are the same, requiring step-handling to meet each of the changing emotions:

- Immobilisation
- Denial
- Anger
- Bargaining

- Depression
- Testing
- Acceptance

PREPARING FOR CHANGE

PEOPLE

POSITIVE RESPONSE

Even those in favour of the change - such as those starting a new job, those about to be married, those moving home and (NB: change managers) those on secondment to projects - will need managing to ensure that they do not succumb to pessimism as they move through the different phases.

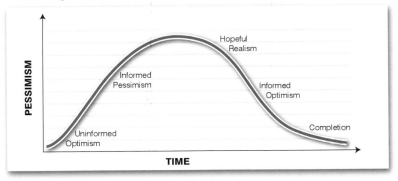

PREPARING FOR CHANGE

PEOPLE

POSITIVE RESPONSE

Reactions will be different at each phase of the change programme:

Uninformed optimism: People are self-confident and positive towards the change

Informed pessimism: People start exhibiting negative responses to change; lose confidence

Hopeful realism: People start to see achievability of change; confidence starts growing

Informed optimism: Confidence returns; people throw themselves into project

Completion: People help rest of organisation; give out confidence

ORGANISATIONAL READINESS TO CHANGE

- Change is difficult; before starting a change programme, it makes sense to assess just how difficult it will be to push through

- The culture of an organisation will affect the ability and speed of an organisation to accept change

- To change an organisation you must change the people, their beliefs and attitudes and their ways of working; this can be very difficult, especially in strong cultures and often in successful companies (no burning platform)

- It is, therefore, important to understand the readiness of the organisation and management to change

ORGANISATIONAL READINESS TO CHANGE

When considering a change programme there are three objectives*:

- **Unfreezing** the current state of affairs
- **Transition** to the new state
- **Re-freezing** or stabilising the changes to make them permanent

*Kurt Lewin (1951)

ORGANISATIONAL READINESS TO CHANGE

FORCE FIELD ANALYSIS

- This is a useful technique which identifies the forces pushing the change and those resisting
- These forces can be weighted, helping you to see where the balance lies – and its viability – and therefore what you need to do to address the balance to ensure success – if you can!

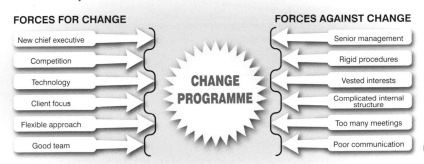

FORCES FOR CHANGE

- New chief executive
- Competition
- Technology
- Client focus
- Flexible approach
- Good team

CHANGE PROGRAMME

FORCES AGAINST CHANGE

- Senior management
- Rigid procedures
- Vested interests
- Complicated internal structure
- Too many meetings
- Poor communication

PREPARING FOR CHANGE

EXAMPLE 1

A major change programme is about to be initiated in a company. The key steps to be taken up to the announcement would be:

- Prepare a communications plan
- Develop questions and answers for managers to use when briefing their staff
- Inform major stakeholders
- Brief managers and inform them of the timing of the cascade of information down the layers of the organisation
- Issue press release (if appropriate)
- Issue communication to everyone

PREPARING FOR CHANGE

EXAMPLE 2

An employee has just been seconded to a change programme from her normal job. She is likely to experience a range of emotions when told:

- Elation at being chosen coupled with fear for her future role post-project
- Concern at the responsibility
- Anxiety about her current reporting relationships
- Lack of certainty regarding her role
- Possible worries about her ability

These concerns can be handled by the current superior giving the individual a proper briefing, explaining that the secondment represents a vote of confidence and stressing the importance of the project and role. This would then be reinforced by another briefing from the project director or sponsor.

PREPARING FOR CHANGE

EXAMPLE 3

A company has just been acquired. To ensure a smooth transition period, the acquiring company must immediately issue a communication to all staff setting out the blueprint for the future, ensuring that change is kept aligned with the present culture as much as possible. Specifically the company should:

- Explain any immediate changes to operations
- Set out the longer-term plans
- Stress the benefits that are expected to accrue from the acquisition
- Set up briefing meetings and a channel for communications
- Ensure that concerns are met with as sympathetically as possible under the circumstances
- Ensure that key individuals are personally reasured

MAKING CHANGE HAPPEN

KEY STEPS

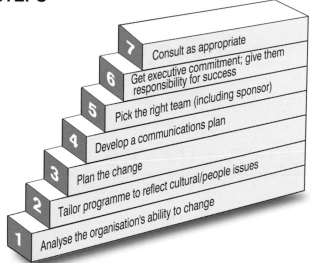

7 Consult as appropriate

6 Get executive commitment; give them responsibility for success

5 Pick the right team (including sponsor)

4 Develop a communications plan

3 Plan the change

2 Tailor programme to reflect cultural/people issues

1 Analyse the organisation's ability to change

CHANGE MANAGEMENT FRAMEWORK

The key to successful change management, as in any project, is **successful planning**.

This means thinking through all the issues, any problems that may arise, the steps and actions necessary to counter them and the team that will be required. If this means getting external help then do not be afraid to do so.

The following pages contain a framework to help in planning a change programme. This can be used for any change programme, no matter how large or small. The differences will be the extent of the change, the complexity of the project and the team required to deliver it.

CHANGE MANAGEMENT FRAMEWORK

This table sets out the key tasks, methods and outputs for a change management programme.

	OBJECTIVES	TASKS	METHODS	OUTPUTS
Analysis (Phase I)	to understand the organisation, its culture and the capacity for change	review: structure, strategy, culture, systems, morale, management practices, external environment	desk research, interviews, workshops, brainstorming	organisational analysis, culture "map", change capacity
Design (Phase II)	to agree the vision, build the team and obtain consensus	develop vision, select team, build buy-in	workshops, meetings, communications	vision, team, consensus, leader/support

70

Table continued ⟶

CHANGE MANAGEMENT FRAMEWORK

	OBJECTIVES	TASKS	METHODS	OUTPUTS
Planning (Phase III)	to plan the realisation of the change	develop plan, build in contingencies, allocate resources, agree timing	desk research, field research, workshops, planning methodologies	plan, risk analysis, dependency chart, agreed resources
Implementation (Phase IV)	to realise the vision by putting the change(s) through the organisation	roll out change across the organisation, communicate to stakeholders, manage risks and dependencies	meetings, actions, team work, workshops, communications	changed organisation, improved performance, survival, changed culture

71

MAKING CHANGE HAPPEN

CHANGE MANAGEMENT FRAMEWORK

PHASE I - ANALYSIS

- In this phase it is necessary to understand the nature of the change as well as the culture of the organisation and its capacity to absorb change (many organisations are now complaining of change overload)

- This will involve carrying out staff surveys, analysing past projects, reviewing the structure, strategy management styles and finally the interactions with external third parties

Output

- The output from this phase is an understanding of the organisation as it relates to the project and a 'map' of the culture

- This should enable you to plan to avoid the potential pitfalls which could arise in the next phase

- Having assessed the change capacity, the pace and scale of change can be optimised

CHANGE MANAGEMENT FRAMEWORK

PHASE II - DESIGN

- In this phase of the project the programme is designed; this should be undertaken at a high level and will involve agreeing the precise nature of the vision, building the team to implement the changes and starting to get buy-in from personnel

- The champion should also be agreed at this stage prior to detailed planning; communication, workshops and discussions are critical at this point

Output

- Is a framework for managing change and includes shared vision, team building and agreed responsibilities

MAKING CHANGE HAPPEN

CHANGE MANAGEMENT FRAMEWORK

PHASE III - PLANNING

- The objective here is to plan the realisation of the change in detail; this requires looking to the future and thinking through all the risks, dependencies, contingencies and potential problems, and putting together a plan to address them all

- This would include allocating resources, agreeing timing, analysing implications and obtaining buy-in in principle from those affected by talking to them and getting their input

Output

- Will include plans, risk analysis, dependency chart and resources to achieve the plan

MAKING CHANGE HAPPEN

CHANGE MANAGEMENT FRAMEWORK
PHASE IV - IMPLEMENTATION

- Having put the plan together you must now implement it
- This means ensuring that the plan is followed but that it is re-evaluated as appropriate in the light of changes to the operating environment and/or strategy and because things crop up which were not foreseen
- The critical skills here are project management and diplomacy; better management of the previous stages will make this stage that much easier

Output

- A well managed and successful change programme, leading to a *better organisation*; well positioned for the future

IMPLEMENTATION PLAN EXAMPLE

PROJECT	JUN	JUL	AUG	SEP	OCT	NOV	DEC	JAN	FEB	MAR	APR	MAY
MOBILISATION												
CHANGE MANAGEMENT (Change management line expanded to demonstrate some key activities)												
Agree communication strategy												
Issue communications												
Agree team												
Hold initial briefing meetings												
Hold workshops												
Re-evaluate change plan												
Make changes and re-brief as necessary												
INFORMATION TECHNOLOGY												
RESTRUCTURE TREASURY												
GL / MIS / BUDGETING												
PROCESS IMPROVEMENTS												
DISTRIBUTION CHANNELS												
"HOUSEKEEPING"												
RE-ENGINEER NEW PRODUCT DEVELOPMENT												
MARKETING												
PROGRESS MEETINGS	☆	☆	☆	☆	☆	☆	☆	☆	☆	☆	☆	☆

MAKING CHANGE HAPPEN

IMPLEMENTATION PLAN

The chart on the previous page shows how change management fits in with a programme and how it is supportive of the larger goals.

Such goals may be to implement: a new IT infrastructure; a radically new organisation; redesigned process; etc.

Whatever the change, it is necessary to integrate the change management into the overall programme, not forgetting 'business as usual'.

COMMITMENT

- The table on the next page indicates the key levels of commitment that determine whether a change programme is a success or a failure, on a scale of 1 to 5 where 1 is total failure and 5 total success

- You must have the commitment of both management and staff for success; but their cooperation is never guaranteed and can range from resistance; through passive non-resistance but not helping; assistance, and finally a true commitment to making it happen

- Without commitment from both management and staff the programme will fail – any programme that falls on the line of resistance from either party has little or no chance of success – or will require a massive effort to get it there

- The objective of successful change management is to move programmes away from the bottom left quartile [1] and towards the top right [5]

OBTAINING COMMITMENT

It is vital to have both staff and executive commitment to any change for it to be successful. (2 or less: forget; 4 or above: success; 3: needs work).

MAKING CHANGE HAPPEN

TEAM MANAGEMENT

A small dedicated team to manage change will have a major effect on an organisation which will be disproportionate to the size of the team. Selecting the correct balance of individuals is therefore critical.

'Give me a lever long enough and a fulcrum on which to place it, and I shall move the world.'
Archimedes

Change team

Change agents

Organisation

TEAM MANAGEMENT

ROLES

Several roles are critical to successful change management. Select the right people or the project will fail. Team numbers will vary depending on project size and duration, but some key factors are:

- A senior executive must visibly sponsor the project

- A senior person must take day-to-day responsibility

- A full-time project manager with experience of managing change must run the project (often a role for external consultants)

- The team must have the correct skills and understanding

TEAM MANAGEMENT

ROLES

- Include people with knowledge of the organisation and those with experience of change programmes (external consultants often involved too)
- Sufficient people at all levels in the organisations must be 'Ambassadors of Progress', and/or change agents
- Outside consultants can often act as useful catalysts because of their independence

Test proposed team members for appropriateness using some of the many methods available (Belbin, 16PF, Myers-Briggs, ODR, etc). This ensures the correct blend of skills. See the *Psychometric Testing Pocketbook*.

MAKING CHANGE HAPPEN

CHANGE TEAM DEVELOPMENT

A change project will require a project team.

It will be focussed on a single primary (or fundamental) objective – to effect the change. Of course, it will have several subsidiary (or means) objectives.

In order to succeed the team will need a blend of skills and experience coupled with knowledge of the organisation. It must, therefore, be drawn from across the organisation and will be cross-functional.

See the diagram following.

CHANGE TEAM DEVELOPMENT

To form the cross-functional team it will mean taking staff, temporarily, out of line roles (where they are comfortable) and putting them into a different structure, possibly with ad hoc reporting lines where status or grade is irrelevant. Team members should be innovative as they will be tasked with managing problems not functions.

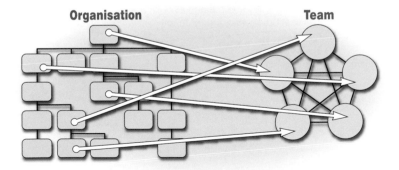

MAKING CHANGE HAPPEN

TEAM MANAGEMENT
DEVELOPMENT PROCESS*

The four development stages that teams go through are generally recognised as follows:

FORMING
Still a group of individuals; each is trying to set their mark on the group

PERFORMING
Previous three stages have to be completed first; very little effective group work will happen until this stage, although individuals may contribute well

STORMING
A period of conflict as members get to know each other, egos are bruised and dynamic interplay takes place (needs careful handling to make sure that it is constructive not destructive)

NORMING
Following the conflict of the previous stage, the group norms and modus operandi are now established

Team members rarely work well together from day one and have to go through a process of finding out about each other and achieving a working understanding. Only then will they deliver. The earlier teams form, the quicker they move into productive performance.

* After Tuckman

REACTIONS TO CHANGE

Resistance is almost inherent in people – whether they display it openly or not. The challenge of change is to move the organisation and its people down the scale, overcoming resistance. From defiance – through compliance – to alliance.

The challenge is to move the organisation and people down the scale.

DEFIANCE	Against change covertly/overtly
COMPLIANCE	Goes along with it, but grudgingly
ALLIANCE	Supports

RESISTANCE

When you come to implement the changes, no matter what you have done to prepare the ground, it will still come as a surprise to many people.

This surprise will turn into resistance quickly and must be managed to ensure success.

Resistance is a vote for the status quo and must be dealt with to prevent disruptive behaviour. It must be planned for and handled well, otherwise it will get worse and could damage the project.

Address people's fears to gain their commitment.

RESISTANCE

Resistance occurs from:

- Uncertainty
- Loss of control
- Fear of the difference
- Loss of power
- Loss of status
- Increased workloads
- Threat
- Misunderstandings

MAKING CHANGE HAPPEN

RESISTANCE
HOW TO DEAL WITH IT

- Involve people in the change process
- Train them appropriately
- Communicate – and explain the changes in easy to understand terms
- Deal with their perception of threats and concerns
- Develop shared vision and buy-in
- Address the concerns of key stakeholders

Successful change management is about overcoming resistance.

MAKING CHANGE HAPPEN

RESISTANCE

To deal with resistance it is helpful to identify where stakeholders sit. These can be classified into nine categories* with increasing levels of resistance:

1. Partners   – who support your agenda

2. Allies   – who will support you given encouragement

3. Fellow travellers   – are passive supporters and may be committed to the agenda but not to you or the team personally

4. Bedfellows   – who support the agenda but do not trust you or the team

5. Fence-sitters   – whose feelings are unclear

* *Gerard Egan (1994)*

MAKING CHANGE HAPPEN

RESISTANCE

6. Loose cannons   – are dangerous as they may oppose issues where they have no direct interest

7. Opponents   – who oppose the agenda but not you or the team personally

8. Adversaries   – who oppose the agenda and you and the team personally

9. The voiceless   – stakeholders who will be affected but have little power to oppose or support and lack advocates

Each category needs to be addressed differently - partners and allies kept on side, opponents converted, and adversaries marginalised and discredited.

RESISTANCE

GAINING ACCEPTANCE

Gaining acceptance goes through the process below, starting with those who are most likely to accept change – innovators – until finally the laggards are won over – or leave.

Use the innovators as Ambassadors of Progress.

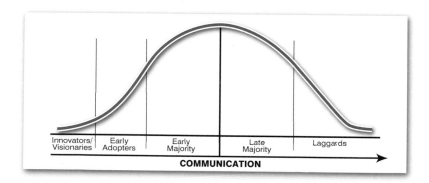

COMFORT ZONES

People's fears (real or imagined) need to be understood by management and this involves entering the **Zone of Uncomfortable Debate (ZOUD)***. This is about taking the arguments out of managers' comfort zones **(Zone of Comfortable Debate, ZOCD)** - where they are happy to discuss issues and questions that are peripheral to the real problems - and into the uncomfortable zone (ZOUD) to discuss sensitive and emotional issues.

ZOCD

ZOUD

Core assumptions

> The closer that you get to core beliefs and feelings the more difficult it is to discuss changes. This may have to be carried out informally but must be done to obtain buy in.

Increasing emotion/sensitivity

* C. Bowman

(93)

'Corporate America is littered
with the wreckage of technically sound
programmes that have been crushed by employee
resistance to change.'
Tom Terez – Modern Management

COMMUNICATION

COMMUNICATION

THE FIVE Ws

Who should be told?

When should they be told?

What should they be told?

Which form(s) of media to use?

Where should control of communication sit?

Develop a communications plan!

THE FIVE Ws

Addressing the **five Ws** is an essential element of a change programme. Poor communication means that the wrong message can go out, or be badly timed, misunderstood or just missed. This can lead to resistance, antipathy and failure.

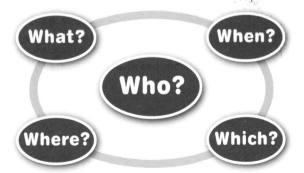

THE FIVE Ws

WHO?

- Everyone who needs to be told about something should be told

- Openness is the key (although there will always be some things which are not disseminated as widely as others)

COMMUNICATION

THE FIVE Ws
WHEN?

- Project members must be briefed prior to them joining the project
- All affected employees should be told at the same time, to avoid spread of rumours
- Brief those internally before those externally; you don't want staff finding out about change from the media
- Make an announcement following a significant event or decision
- Follow any legal requirements – eg consultation/TUPE

THE FIVE Ws
WHAT?

The four rules of communication are:

> **Tell 'em when you have something to say**
>
> **Tell 'em what you plan to do**
>
> **Tell 'em what you are doing**
>
> **Tell 'em what you will be doing**

COMMUNICATION

THE FIVE Ws
WHICH?

- Choose the most effective vehicle to get your message across

- This could be via seminars, one-to-ones, email, cascade briefings, press releases, etc. The key is to make sure that your message is timely and goes out to the right people, in the right way, to avoid rumours and hearsay

THE FIVE Ws
WHERE?

Where should control of the communication process sit?

Usually communications will be under the control of the sponsoring executive.
For a large programme, this is usually the CEO.

It is such an important part of the programme's success that it MUST NOT be left to a junior.

- The project manager will normally have input into it
- Personnel will usually be consulted
- The corporate communications people, if appropriate, will be involved

EPILOGUE

HOW TO SUCCEED

Success in Change Management involves being **SMART**:

Strategy defined

Management buy-in

Assurance to staff

Risk analysis

Time critical implementation

HOW TO FAIL

Change Management will fail when you are **STUPID**:

Sponsorship not forthcoming

Team members do not function as agents of change

Unclear vision and commitment

Poorly planned change programme

Inappropriate/insufficient communication

Don't take account of culture

TIPS

Confrontation
Avoid confrontation; obtain a consensus

Manpower changes
Changes in manpower (which often result from change) must be dealt with sympathetically to ensure buy-in and acceptance as well as good morale for remaining staff

Above all communicate!

BALLOT SLIP

Change ....

No Change ......

EPILOGUE

TIPS

Automation
Bear in mind that automation usually results in manual positions being made redundant

Co-operation and buy-in
It is important that buy-in is obtained from staff by consensus and not imposition

FURTHER READING

Communications Pocketbook,
By Seán Mistéil, published by Management Pocketbooks

Decision Making Pocketbook,
By Neil Russell-Jones, published by Management Pocketbooks

Handling Resistance Pocketbook,
By Mike Clayton, published by Management Pocketbooks

Organizational Behaviour – an introductory text,
By Andrzej Huczynski and David Buchanan Published by FT Prentice Hall

Strategy Pocketbook,
By Neil Russell-Jones, published by Management Pocketbooks

Tackling Difficult Conversations Pocketbook,
By Peter English, published by Management Pocketbook

Understanding Organizations,
By Charles Handy, published by Pelican

Pocketbooks – *available in both paperback and digital formats*

360 Degree Feedback
Absence Management
Appraisals
Assertiveness
Balance Sheet
Business Planning
Call Centre Customer Care
Career Transition
Coaching
Cognitive Behavioural Coaching
Communicator's
Competencies
Creative Manager's
C.R.M.
Cross-cultural Business
Customer Service
Decision-making
Delegation
Developing People
Discipline & Grievance
Diversity
Emotional Intelligence
Employment Law
Empowerment
Energy and Well-being
Facilitator's
Feedback

Flexible Workplace
Handling Complaints
Handling Resistance
Icebreakers
Impact & Presence
Improving Efficiency
Improving Profitability
Induction
Influencing
International Trade
Interviewer's
I.T. Trainer's
Key Account Manager's
Leadership
Learner's
Management Models
Manager's
Managing Assessment Centres
Managing Budgets
Managing Cashflow
Managing Change
Managing Customer Service
Managing Difficult Participants
Managing Recruitment
Managing Upwards
Managing Your Appraisal
Marketing

Meetings
Memory
Mentoring
Motivation
Negotiator's
Networking
NLP
Nurturing Innovation
Openers & Closers
People Manager's
Performance Management
Personal Success
Positive Mental Attitude
Presentations
Problem Behaviour
Problem Solving
Project Management
Psychometric Testing
Resolving Conflict
Reward
Sales Excellence
Salesperson's
Self-managed Development
Starting In Management
Strategy
Stress
Succeeding at Interviews

Tackling Difficult Conversations
Talent Management
Teambuilding Activities
Teamworking
Telephone Skills
Telesales
Thinker's
Time Management
Trainer's
Training Evaluation
Training Needs Analysis
Transfer of Learning
Virtual Teams
Vocal Skills
Working Relationships
Workplace Politics

Pocketfiles

Trainer's Blue Pocketfile of
Ready-to-use Activities

Trainer's Green Pocketfile of
Ready-to-use Activities

Trainer's Red Pocketfile of
Ready-to-use Activities

20.07.11